CHIEF JOSEPH

by Laura K. Murray

PEBBLE
a capstone imprint

Pebble Explore is published by Pebble, an imprint of Capstone.
1710 Roe Crest Drive
North Mankato, Minnesota 56003
www.capstonepub.com

Library of Congress Cataloging-in-Publication Data
Names: Murray, Laura K., 1989– author.
Title: Chief Joseph / Laura K. Murray.
Description: North Mankato : Pebble, 2021. | Series: Biographies | Includes bibliographical references. | Audience: Ages 6–8 | Audience: Grades 2–3 | Summary: "How much do you know about Chief Joseph? Find out the facts you need to know about this leader of the Nez Perce people. You'll learn about the early life, challenges, and major accomplishments of this important American"—Provided by publisher.
Identifiers: LCCN 2020025158 (print) | LCCN 2020025159 (ebook) | ISBN 9781977132031 (library binding) | ISBN 9781977133052 (trade paperback)| ISBN 9781977153982 (pdf)
Subjects: LCSH: Joseph, Nez Percé chief, 1840–1904—Juvenile literature. | Nez Percé Indians—Kings and rulers—Biography—Juvenile literature. | Nez Percé Indians—Wars, 1877—Juvenile literature.
Classification: LCC E99.N5 M87 2021 (print) | LCC E99.N5 (ebook) | DDC 979.004/9741240092 [B]—dc23
LC record available at https://lccn.loc.gov/2020025158
LC ebook record available at https://lccn.loc.gov/2020025159

Image Credits
Alamy: Abbus Acastra, 9, nik wheeler, 24; Bridgeman Images: © Look and Learn, 17; Getty Images: Stock Montage, 8, Universal Images Group/Prisma by Dukas, 11; Library of Congress: cover, 1, 6, 15, 18, 19, 20, 23, 27; The Metropolitan Museum of Art: Gilman Collection, Museum Purchase, 2005, 12; National Park Service: Nez Perce National Historical Park, 26; The New York Public Library: 22; North Wind Picture Archives: 7, 16; Shutterstock: Curly Pat (geometric background), cover, back cover, 2, 29, Jennifer Bosvert, 25; Smithsonian Institution: National Portrait Gallery, 5, 29

Editorial Credits
Editor: Erika L. Shores; Designer: Elyse White; Media Researcher: Svetlana Zhurkin; Production Specialist: Spencer Rosio

All internet sites appearing in back matter were available and accurate when this book was sent to press.

Table of Contents

Words in **bold** are in the glossary.

Who Was Chief Joseph?

Chief Joseph was a leader of the Nez Perce people. He wanted the Nez Perce to be treated fairly. But the U.S. **government** forced the Nez Perce people out of their lands.

The Nez Perce War of 1877 was one of many major conflicts between American Indians and the U.S. Army. Chief Joseph led his people during their **retreat**. The U.S. Army was much bigger. But the Nez Perce kept fighting. Chief Joseph became a voice for his people.

Growing Up

Joseph was born March 3, 1840, in Wallowa Valley. Today, the land is part of the United States. It is in northeastern Oregon. At that time, the Wallowa **band** of Nez Perce lived there.

Nez Perce mothers put their babies in cradleboards. They carried them on their backs.

American Indian boys took part in horse races to show their skills and bravery.

Joseph's American Indian name was Hin-mah-too-yah-lat-kekt. It meant "Thunder Rolling Down the Mountain." But most people knew him as Joseph or Joseph the Younger. His father was called Old Joseph or Joseph the Elder. Joseph had six brothers and sisters.

a group of Nez Perce meeting with a settler

When Joseph was young, white people began moving onto Nez Perce land. The white settlers and the Indians were friendly at first. Then many more settlers came. They brought sickness, alcohol, and guns.

Old Joseph helped keep peace. He made treaties with the U.S. government. One of these agreements said the Nez Perce could keep lands from the Wallowa Valley into Washington and Idaho forever.

Nez Perce and government leaders meeting in 1855

Keeping Their Lands

In 1860, settlers found gold in the Nez Perce land. Thousands of settlers rushed to get the gold. The U.S. government broke its promises. The Nez Perce were forced to give up their lands.

The government wanted the Nez Perce to move out of the Wallowa Valley. They would be sent to a small **reservation** in Idaho. Old Joseph would not agree. He no longer trusted the government.

an engraving of Old Joseph

Chief Joseph led his people after his father's death.

In 1871, Old Joseph died. Before he died, he told his son to lead their people. He said never to sell their lands. Young Joseph was 31 years old. He became known as Chief Joseph. For years, he and the Nez Perce would not move.

In May 1877, the U.S. government said the Nez Perce had 30 days to move. If they did not, the army would attack. Chief Joseph did not want war. He agreed to go to Idaho.

A Strong Leader

Chief Joseph and the Nez Perce got ready to leave for Idaho. Other bands joined them. The group had about 700 men, women, and children. Fewer than 200 were warriors.

Before they got to the reservation, war broke out. In June 1877, young Nez Perce warriors killed 18 settlers. They were upset at being treated unfairly. Settlers had killed their families. A few days later, the U.S. Army attacked the Nez Perce. The Nez Perce won. It was the first battle in the Nez Perce War.

Nez Perce women hiding during a battle

U.S. troops followed the Nez Perce for several months.

Over the next four months, the Nez Perce traveled through Oregon, Washington, Idaho, and Montana. The U.S. Army sent 2,000 troops after them. The army had more weapons. But the Nez Perce won battles or got away. They knew the lands. They were skilled horsemen and fighters. Chief Joseph's younger brother led the warriors. His name was Ollokot.

The Nez Perce looked for help. They went to the Crow nation in Montana. But the Crow people would not help them. Then they went north toward Canada. The Lakota people lived there.

The Nez Perce went through the mountains in freezing weather.

Fighting to Go Home

By October 1877, the Nez Perce were in the Bear Paw Mountains in northern Montana. They were just 40 miles (64 kilometers) away from Canada. But they were tired. They were hungry and freezing. As many as 200 Nez Perce had died. Ollokot was one of them.

The Battle of Bear Paw was the last battle of the war.

Chief Joseph surrendered after months of resistance.

On October 5, 1877, Chief Joseph **surrendered**. He was 37 years old. He said his heart was sick and sad. He said, "I will fight no more forever."

The U.S. Army arrested Chief Joseph.

The U.S. government told Chief Joseph they could go home. Instead, the Nez Perce were taken to Kansas as prisoners. Then they were sent to a reservation in Oklahoma. Many died of sickness there.

Chief Joseph kept working to get his people home. In 1879, he went to Washington, D.C. He met with U.S. President Rutherford B. Hayes. Chief Joseph said all men are brothers. He said there would be peace if all people were treated the same. Still the Nez Perce were not able to go home.

Nez Perce were forced to live on reservations.

In 1885, the government let the Nez Perce go back to the northwest. But many of them had to live on the Colville Reservation. It was in northern Washington.

Chief Joseph did not stop speaking out for equal **rights**. Later he spoke with presidents William McKinley and Theodore Roosevelt. He was never able to go home to the Wallowa Valley.

Chief Joseph died on September 21, 1904. He was 64 years old. He was buried on the Colville Reservation. His doctor said he had died of a broken heart.

Chief Joseph around 1900

Remembering Chief Joseph

Today, the Chief Joseph band of Nez Perce lives in Washington. There is a town called Joseph in Wallowa County, Oregon. It celebrates Chief Joseph Days. **Powwows** are named for Chief Joseph in Idaho, Montana, and other states.

Chief Joseph Days parade in Joseph, Oregon

Joseph Canyon

Many places are named for Chief Joseph. Chief Joseph Pass is between Idaho and Montana. Joseph Canyon is in Oregon and Washington. The Chief Joseph Dam is on Washington's Columbia River.

Today, people can walk the Nez Perce National Historic Trail. It goes 1,170 miles (1,883 km) from Oregon to Montana. The trail marks the retreat of Chief Joseph's people. It shows important places in Nez Perce history. They are part of the Nez Perce National Historical Park.

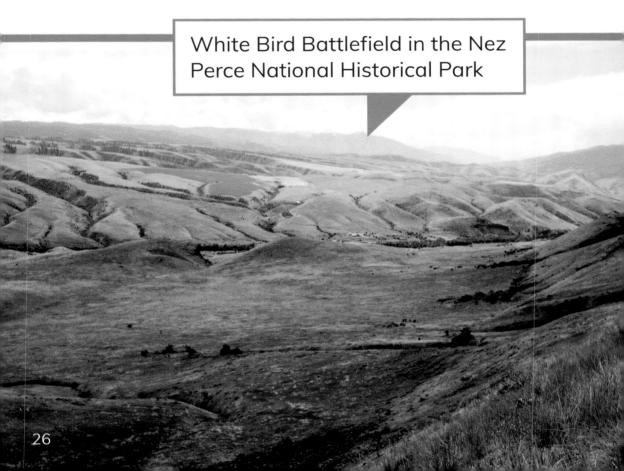

White Bird Battlefield in the Nez Perce National Historical Park

Chief Joseph became famous during his life. He gave hope to his people. He wanted peace. He never stopped fighting for the rights of American Indians. People will remember him forever.

Important Dates

Date	Event
March 3, 1840	Chief Joseph is born in Wallowa Valley in northeastern Oregon.
1871	Young Joseph becomes Chief Joseph.
May 1877	U.S. forces give the Nez Perce 30 days to move to the Idaho reservation.
June 1877	Nez Perce warriors kill 18 white settlers. The U.S. Army attacks the Nez Perce.
June–October 1877	The Nez Perce retreat for more than 1,400 miles (2,250 km).
October 5, 1877	Chief Joseph surrenders.
1878	The Nez Perce are forced to live at a reservation in Oklahoma.
1879	Chief Joseph meets with U.S. President Rutherford B. Hayes in Washington, D.C.
1885	Nez Perce arrive at the Colville Reservation in Washington.
September 21, 1904	Chief Joseph dies at Colville Reservation at age 64.

Fast Facts

Name:
Chief Joseph

Role:
leader of the Nez Perce

Life dates:
March 3, 1840 to September 21, 1904

Key accomplishments:
Chief Joseph and his people had one of the most famous retreats in history. The U.S. Army had many more people and weapons. For nearly four months, the Nez Perce won fights or got away. Chief Joseph never stopped fighting for the rights of his people to go home.

Glossary

band (BAND)—a community of American Indians who share leadership or government

government (GUHV-urn-muhnt)—the group of people who make rules and decisions for a country or state

powwow (POW-wow)—an American Indian celebration

reservation (rez-er-VAY-shuhn)—an area of land where American Indians moved after having to give up their homelands

retreat (ri-TREET)—the moving back or withdrawal from a difficult situation

right (RITE)—something that everyone should be able to do or have and that the government shouldn't be able to take away, such as the right to speak freely

surrender (suh-REN-dur)—to give up

Read More

Schwartz, Heather E. *Seeking Freedom: Causes and Effects of the Flight of the Nez Perce.* North Mankato, MN: Capstone Press, 2015.

Strand, Jennifer. *Chief Joseph.* Minneapolis: Abdo Zoom, 2018.

Internet Sites

Chief Joseph: American History for Kids
www.americanhistoryforkids.com/chief-joseph/

Chief Joseph
www.ducksters.com/history/native_americans/chief_joseph.php

National Park Service: Lake Roosevelt: Chief Joseph
www.nps.gov/laro/learn/historyculture/chief-joseph.htm

Index

MW01155210